Go Outside!

GO FISHING!

By Peter Finn

Gareth Stevens
PUBLISHING

Please visit our website, www.garethstevens.com. For a free color catalog of all our high-quality books, call toll free 1-800-542-2595 or fax 1-877-542-2596.

Library of Congress Cataloging-in-Publication Data

Names: Finn, Peter, 1978- author.
Title: Go fishing! / Peter Finn.
Description: New York : Gareth Stevens Publishing, [2020] | Series: Go outside! | Includes index.
Identifiers: LCCN 2019009907| ISBN 9781538244814 (paperback) | ISBN 9781538244838 (library bound) | ISBN 9781538244821 (6 pack)
Subjects: LCSH: Fishing–Juvenile literature.
Classification: LCC SH445 .F56 2020 | DDC 639.2–dc23
LC record available at https://lccn.loc.gov/2019009907

Published in 2020 by
Gareth Stevens Publishing
111 East 14th Street, Suite 349
New York, NY 10003

Copyright © 2020 Gareth Stevens Publishing

Editor: Therese Shea
Designer: Sarah Liddell

Photo credits: Cover, p. 1 Africa Studio/Shutterstock.com; p. 5 patat/Shutterstock.com; pp. 7, 24 (fishing rod) PointImages/Shutterstock.com; p. 9 Joe Belanger/Shutterstock.com; p. 11 vitec/Shutterstock.com; p. 13 PhotoChur/Shutterstock.com; p. 15 Rocksweeper/Shutterstock.com; pp. 17, 24 (bobber) iyd39/Shutterstock.com; pp. 19, 24 (trout) HABRDA/Shutterstock.com; p. 21 Monkey Business Images/Shutterstock.com; p. 23 Sergey Novikov/Shutterstock.com.

Printed in the United States of America

Some of the images in this book illustrate individuals who are models. The depictions do not imply actual situations or events.

CPSIA compliance information: Batch #CW20GS: For further information contact Gareth Stevens, New York, New York at 1-800-542-2595.

Contents

My name is Cat.
I love to fish!

This is my fishing rod.

At the end of the line is a hook.
That's where I put the bait.

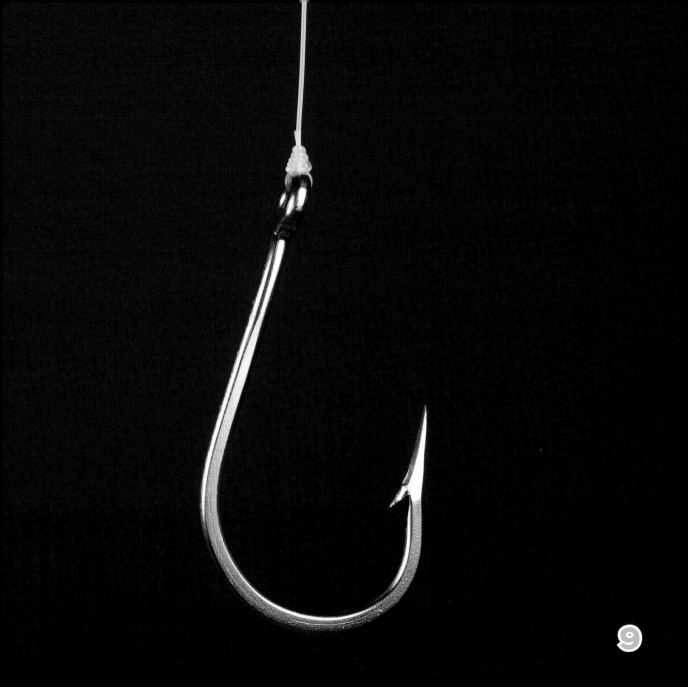

9

I use worms for bait.
These are called
nightcrawlers!

I fish in rivers.
I fish in lakes, too.

I stay still while
I wait for a fish.
I don't want to
scare the fish.

The bobber moves.
I feel a fish on
my hook!

I caught a fish!
It's called a trout.

Fishing is fun
with family.
It's fun with
friends, too!

Fishing is fun
for everyone!
Go fishing!

Words to Know

bobber   fishing rod   trout

Index